A Very Merry

Swiftmas

Holiday Coloring Fun

We hope you enjoy this coloring book! Please don't forget to leave us a review on Amazon. It would really help us out a lot. When you leave your review please feel free to share your colorful creations. We would love to see them.
Thank you.
We appreciate it! :)

Wishing You a Merry Swiftmas,

Color Haven Press

COLOR YOURSELF CALM!

In today's fast-paced world, prioritizing mental wellness is more important than ever. The challenges of recent years have shown us just how essential it is to find moments of peace, and for many, immersing in art has become a wonderful way to nurture self-care, bringing joy and serenity into our lives.

OUR PAPER CHOICE

We've opted for standard quality paper to keep our books affordable, given the limited paper options available on Amazon. To prevent any bleed-through from markers or pens, we recommend placing a blank sheet of thicker paper behind the page you're coloring. Thank you for your understanding and for making the most of each page!

SHOW OFF YOUR COLORING

Since our books launched on Amazon, we've loved seeing them come to life through the creativity of colorists like you! Feel free to share photos of your finished pages in your reviews to showcase your unique style and inspire others. We can't wait to see your beautiful work!

This Book Belongs To

_____

_____

_____

Printed in Great Britain
by Amazon